You are here.

★ **YOU ARE HERE.**

Let the map lead the way.
Let the dove fly ahead.

On the path.
To the dream.
To the words.
And the songs.

Take the road. Come along.
With Martin and Mahalia.

Martin & Mahalia

HIS WORDS • HER SONG

BY ANDREA DAVIS PINKNEY

ILLUSTRATED BY BRIAN PINKNEY

LITTLE, BROWN AND COMPANY

New York   Boston

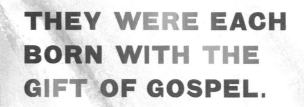

THEY WERE EACH BORN WITH THE GIFT OF GOSPEL.

On Sundays at Ebenezer Baptist Church in Atlanta, Georgia, Martin learned to deliver a sermon, just like his grandfather, the Reverend A.D. Williams, and his daddy, the Reverend Martin Luther King Sr.

Martin wasn't old enough to be a preacher, but even as a boy, he had a **BIG** way of speaking. He learned this from watching his father address the congregation.

Martin's voice kept people in their seats but also sent their praises soaring.

SAME FOR MAHALIA. HER VOICE WAS STRONG-STRONG.

She sang in the choir at Mount Moriah Baptist Church, in the Black Pearl neighborhood of New Orleans, Louisiana. The congregation at Mount Moriah saw Mahalia's gospel gift right away. So did Mahalia's aunt Duke, who was raising her.

That girl could sure **SING.**
She was a jewel in Black Pearl.

Mahalia's gospel gift could move people, too.

With Martin's sermons and Mahalia's songs, folks were free to shout, to sing their joy.

But in the South, where Martin and Mahalia lived,
Jim Crow laws made sure things were not as free.

These laws said:

BLACK

FOLKS

HERE.

        WHITE

        FOLKS

        THERE.

That's how life was for young Martin and Mahalia.
Separate but nowhere near equal.

As he grew, Martin traveled to churches with his family.

Martin **SPOKE** the gospel.

PRAYED the gospel.

SOUGHT the gospel.

TAUGHT the gospel.

Martin preached wherever he went. Anyplace the gospel would be greeted with an **AMEN**.

Martin got to be known as a master minister. His sermons were solid. It wasn't long before many people followed Martin's words.

Through Martin, they had **FOUND THE GOSPEL.**

As *she* grew, Mahalia's voice led her to many different churches.

She **SANG** the gospel.

WORKED the gospel.

LED the gospel.

SPREAD the gospel.

By the time she was grown, record companies called on Mahalia to record her music. Radio stations played her gospel gift.

All kinds of folks, black and white, loved Mahalia's singing. All types of people embraced her music. Mahalia's voice was **BRASS AND BUTTER.** Strong and smooth at the same time.

Mahalia recorded a song called "Move On Up a Little Higher."
She used her gospel gift to **CLAIM THAT SONG.**

FILLED the notes with tones so round.

PULLED the backbeat.

STRETCHED the downbeat.

PUSHED past the boundaries of

HERE AND NOW.

The song sold nearly two million records and put Mahalia Jackson on the map.
When Martin heard "Move On Up a Little Higher," he knew Mahalia could inspire.
Her voice had the power to call folks forward. Martin hoped that together their gospel gifts
could set people on the path to peace.

Mahalia had her eyes on the very same prize. Martin's oratory stirred something deep
inside her. His mighty way of speaking sparked her soul.

Martin's sermons and Mahalia's spirituals
told their listeners:

★ **YOU ARE HERE.**

ON THE PATH.
COME ALONG.

STEP PROUD.
STAND STRONG.

BE BRAVE.
GO WITH ME.

To a place,
to a time,
when we all will **BE FREE.**

People listened and believed.

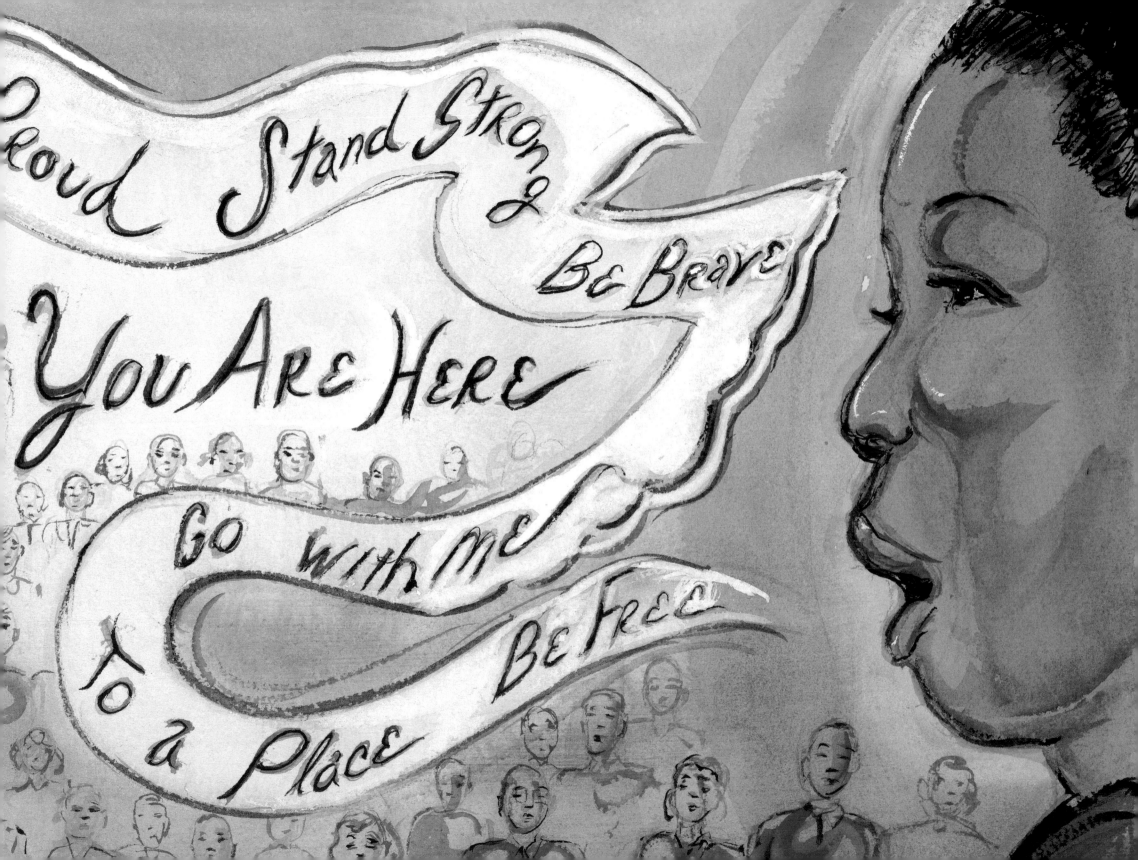

Martin and Mahalia's work together began in 1955 during the Montgomery Bus Boycott, when the people of Montgomery, Alabama, refused to ride city buses.

Martin urged Mahalia to sing while he preached so that the movement could stay on course.

AND, OH, DID SHE SING!

Martin and Mahalia were blazing a trail,
but the fight for justice was far from over.

They wanted to

LIFT their gospel gifts higher.

GROW them bigger.

SHOUT them louder.

Make Americans even **PROUDER.**

Along with several civil rights leaders,
they were excited to take part in the
March on Washington for Jobs and Freedom.

People from all over the nation gathered and
began to make their way toward Washington, D.C.
They traveled on foot, by bus, and on bikes.

They were coming to hear what Martin had to say.
They were eager to listen to Mahalia sing. They
knew where to go. Maps had shown them the way.

This Way to Freedom

TO THE MARCH.
TO THE DREAM.

To a road filled with hope.

TO THE WORDS.
AND THE SONGS.

That would take them to peace.

THIS WAY TO

This way to Freedom
to Freedom
to Freedom

FREEDOM ⟶

The map's marching orders were simple:

THIS WAY TO FREEDOM.

Follow these signs of the times:

CHANGE.
STRENGTH.
UNITY.
LOVE.

Thousands of people met at the foot of the
Washington Monument, where the march began.
Their maps spelled it out:

★ **YOU ARE HERE.**

Many kinds of people stood together with peace in their hearts. They sang "We Shall Overcome" and "Woke Up This Morning with My Mind Stayed on Freedom."

Hecklers hollered:

"WALK ON!"
"GET GONE!"

This didn't stop the marchers.

They were determined to meet violence with nonviolence. Nothing could make them strike back as they followed one another to the Lincoln Memorial, where Mahalia would sing and Martin would preach. While the demonstrators marched, they sang "I'm On My Way."

Martin knew he could not deliver his speech properly until everyone was quiet enough to listen. The moment had come to ask Mahalia for her help.

Mahalia came on strong. She sang a spiritual she knew from church in Black Pearl. She rolled her brass and butter with a

MIGHTY DOSE OF THUNDER.

The crowd settled down.
They were ready to hear Martin.

THE DREAM ⟶

Martin's voice had a force all its own. He started off slowly.

STEADY AS A TRAIN pressing forward.

He began by calling this day the greatest demonstration for freedom in the history of the nation.

Martin told his listeners that now was the time to make justice a reality for all children. This day was a beginning, he said. It was clear that everyone was marching on the path to peace.

"We cannot turn back," Martin proclaimed.

Mahalia's heart filled with pride as Martin's speech swelled to a sermon.

Mahalia called out to her friend,

"TELL THEM ABOUT YOUR DREAM, MARTIN!"

It was Martin's dream that one day his children—and all children—would be judged by the content of their character, not the color of their skin.

There would be no

HERE and **THERE**,

or **US** and **THEM**.

He spoke of the faith that could transform the nation into a beautiful symphony of brotherhood, where everyone could:

WORK TOGETHER.
PRAY TOGETHER.
STAND UP FOR
FREEDOM TOGETHER.

"Let freedom ring!" he declared.
Then, as Martin ended his speech,
some of his listeners joined hands. He roared the
words from an old spiritual: "Free at last, free at last.
Thank God Almighty, we are free at last!"

Mahalia and the crowd of thousands cheered.

The people who had come to hear Martin
on that day were moved to more than a single amen.

It was **AMEN TIMES TEN!**

This was a day
when everyone's voice
was heard.

On the path.
To the dream.

Through **MARTIN'S WORDS**
And **MAHALIA'S SONGS**.

They'd **TAKEN THE ROAD**.
They'd **ALL COME ALONG**.

On the march to be free.
Their intention was clear:

GLORY, HALLELUJAH!

 **WE ARE HERE!**

HIS WORDS

The friendship between Martin Luther King Jr. and Mahalia Jackson is one underscored by the collective influence of their voices. Martin and Mahalia articulated hope at a time when Americans were eager for social change.

Music played an important role in the civil rights movement, and it was Mahalia Jackson's full-bodied contralto that propelled the movement forward. Mahalia, known as the Queen of Gospel, helped bring gospel singing and spirituals to mainstream audiences, increasing the appeal of this type of music traditionally sung in churches.

In 1950, Mahalia was invited to perform at Carnegie Hall. About Mahalia's singing, Martin Luther King Jr. said that a voice like hers comes along once in a millennium. Other notables and dignitaries agreed. Mahalia sang for four presidents: Harry S. Truman, Dwight D. Eisenhower, John F. Kennedy, and Lyndon B. Johnson. President Kennedy ensured that Mahalia was invited to sing at his inaugural gala on January 19, 1961. That same year, President Kennedy asked Martin to join him for a meal at the White House, where Martin told the president about his hope for racial equality.

When it was time for the March on Washington for Jobs and Freedom, Mahalia had already gained the recognition and respect of many.

The March on Washington was one of the largest public demonstrations in the history of American civil rights. The organizers of the march summoned thousands of people together with an eye toward reaching very specific goals. They wanted to force Congress to bring about change by embracing President Kennedy's civil rights legislation. This included the integration of all public schools, job training and placement for all unemployed workers, a law preventing job and housing discrimination, and fair voting practices. As the march was being planned, President Kennedy advised Martin and other civil rights leaders to call it off. He was afraid it would lead to violence.

Road maps, flyers, and other pamphlets served as important tools during the civil rights movement, guiding travelers to marches and rallies, to which they often walked, and showing protesters march routes.

In addition, sponsors of the march provided a booklet titled *Organizing Manual—Final Plans for the March on Washington for Jobs and Freedom*. This guide offered helpful pointers to make the march easier to navigate and sustain. It included travel directions to Washington, D.C., and the march schedule. The map's marching orders cited in this book's

HER SONG

narrative—"This way to freedom. Follow these signs of the times: Change. Strength. Unity. Love."—are my creation, incorporated for poetic purposes.

Before Mahalia sang and Martin delivered his speech at the March on Washington, several notable entertainers led the crowd. The event included musical performances by singers Marian Anderson, Joan Baez, and Bob Dylan. Actor Charlton Heston represented a contingent of artists including Harry Belafonte, Marlon Brando, Diahann Carroll, Ossie Davis, Sammy Davis Jr., Lena Horne, Paul Newman, and Sidney Poitier.

There were also speakers who preceded Martin, including most of the "Big Six," some of the influential civil rights leaders who helped Martin organize the march. In addition to Martin, the Big Six included John Lewis, A. Philip Randolph, Roy Wilkins, and Whitney Young Jr. (James Farmer, who was in a Louisiana prison at the time, had his speech read by Floyd B. McKissick, leader of the Congress of Racial Equality.)

While Mahalia and other notable female singers brought their music to the march, some women supported the march by standing up for justice. Actress and activist Josephine Baker and freedom fighters Daisy Bates and Rosa Parks were among them.

The March on Washington turned out to be one of the most defining events in civil rights history. Sadly, Martin didn't live to see his dream fully realized. In 1968, Mahalia Jackson sang "Take My Hand, Precious Lord" at Dr. King's funeral, after he was assassinated. She delivered the spiritual with the soul-rousing emotion of a true friend.

Four years later, when Mahalia Jackson passed away after suffering heart failure, Martin's wife, Mrs. Coretta Scott King, delivered a eulogy at Mahalia's funeral. She praised Mahalia for being black and proud and beautiful.

It was Mahalia's singing coupled with Martin's powerful oratory that gave Americans reasons to embrace justice and rejoice in the beauty of racial unity.

Andrea Davis Pinkney

PAINTING PARALLELS

On August 28, 1963, when Martin Luther King Jr. and Mahalia Jackson inspired the world at the March on Washington, I blew out two candles on my birthday cake. As a toddler, I didn't know of the tremendous impact these individuals would have on me. I grew up in a home where my parents believed that civil rights and music could work together to bring about social change. As a result, I have embraced the belief that vocal power—whether in the form of a speech or a song—can serve as a guidepost. Along these lines, I was inspired by elements that appear on the actual maps demonstrators followed when participating in the March on Washington.

In rendering the paintings for *Martin & Mahalia*, I drew on the tradition of civil rights and spirituals coming together to form a mighty force. The watercolors I have created for this book are intended to give visual resonance to the collaborative strength brought forth in Martin's oratory and Mahalia's musical prowess.

Words can be very compelling. Even small words—*unity, love*—can inspire. Stirred by these succinct yet commanding expressions of hope, I chose to incorporate the words of Martin and Mahalia into the book's scene compositions, often weaving phrases together in the same way Martin Luther King Jr. and Mahalia Jackson combined their respective vocal gifts to form an unshakable ribbon of faith.

Inspiration also came from the works of social realist painters Ben Shahn and Charles Wilbert White. White's monumental figures celebrate the beauty and strength of African American people and our resilience. Shahn sometimes enhanced his paintings with words that expressed pro-social views. His "love for exactitude" is exhibited in this way. Like White and Shahn, I, too, was striving for paintings that make a powerful, positive statement of the times.

The dove cited in the story also served as visual inspiration. This beautiful bird is shown from several perspectives. It is often implicit in the compositions and sometimes hidden to remind readers that peace can prevail, even when we are met with opposition.

Like the sun piercing the sky on a new day, this book's color palette is bold and bright! I contrasted Martin and Mahalia by employing blues and greens for Martin, reds and oranges for Mahalia. Purples and magentas come into the mix when Martin and Mahalia blend their talents and tenacity. Throughout the illustrations, color is used to deliberately express the joy we can all find in the brilliant legacy of two individuals whose vibrancy continues to shine.

Brian Pinkney

Brian Pinkney

For Further Enjoyment:

Adelman, Bob and Charles Johnson. *Mine Eyes Have Seen: Bearing Witness to the Struggle for Civil Rights*. New York: Time Inc. Home Entertainment Books, 2007.

Altman, Susan. *Extraordinary African-Americans*. New York: Children's Press, 2001.

Bolden, Tonya. *M.L.K.: Journey of a King*. New York: Harry N. Abrams, Inc., 2007.

Branch, Taylor. *Parting the Waters: America in the King Years 1954-1963*. New York: Simon & Schuster Paperbacks, 1988.

Carson, Clayborne; Garrow, David J.; Gill, Gerald; Harding, Vincent; Clark Hine, Darlene. *The Eyes on the Prize Civil Rights Reader*. New York: Viking Penguin, 1991.

Carson, Clayborne; Shepard, Kris. *A Call to Conscience: The Landmark Speeches of Dr. Martin Luther King, Jr*. New York: Warner Books, Inc., 2001.

Cornell, Jean Gay. *Mahalia Jackson: Queen of Gospel Song*. Champaign, IL: Garrard Pub. Co., 1974.

Darden, Bob. *People Get Ready!: A New History of Black Gospel Music*. New York: Continuum, 2004.

Hampton, Henry. *Eyes on the Prize: America's Civil Rights Movement*. Blackside, Inc. DVD. PBS Video, 2006.

Heilbut, Anthony. *The Gospel Sound: Good News and Bad Times*. New Jersey: Limelight Editions, 1997.

Jackson, Jesse. *Make a Joyful Noise Unto the Lord!: The Life of Mahalia Jackson, Queen of Gospel Singers*. New York: T.Y. Crowell, 1974.

Jackson, Mahalia. *Movin' On Up*. New York: Hawthorn Books, 1966.

Jones, Hettie. *Big Star Fallin' Mama: Five Women in Black Music*. New York: Viking Press, 1974.

King, Martin Luther Jr. *I Have a Dream*. New York: Scholastic Press, 1997.

Schwerin, Jules. *Got to Tell It: Mahalia Jackson, Queen of Gospel*. New York: Oxford University Press, 1992.

Tofel, Richard J. *Sounding the Trumpet: The Making of John F. Kennedy's Inaugural Address*. Chicago, IL: Ivan R. Dee, 2005.

Selected Discography:

Jackson, Mahalia. *Bless This House*, New York: Columbia Records, 1956.

Jackson, Mahalia. *Come On, Children, Let's Sing*, New York: Columbia Records, 1960.

Jackson, Mahalia. *Great Songs of Love and Faith*, New York: Columbia Records, 1962.

Jackson, Mahalia. *I Believe*, New York: Columbia Records, 1960.

Jackson, Mahalia. *In the Upper Room*, New York: Apollo Records, 1957.

Jackson, Mahalia. *Let's Pray Together*, CBS Records, 1963.

Jackson, Mahalia. *Mahalia Jackson's Greatest Hits*, New York: Columbia Records, 1963.

Jackson, Mahalia. *Mahalia Jackson Sings the Best-Loved Hymns of Dr. Martin Luther King, Jr.*, CBS Records, 1968.

Jackson, Mahalia. *Mahalia Sings*, New York: Columbia Records, 1966.

Jackson, Mahalia. *Newport 1958*, New York: Columbia Records, 1958.

Jackson, Mahalia. *You'll Never Walk Alone*, CBS Records, 1968.

Acknowledgments:

Thank you, Liza Baker, Patti Ann Harris, and Rebecca Sherman for your heart, soul, and hard work in bringing this book to life. And special thanks to the following individuals and institutions for their research assistance:
Steven Diamond, photo editor; Samuel R. Rubin, Education Specialist, John F. Kennedy Library and Museum; Esther Kohn, Education Specialist, John F. Kennedy Library and Museum; Syracuse University; Jennifer Vilaga; and Elizabeth Segal.

TRAVELING TIME

The road to equality was paved step-by-step through the individual and collective efforts of many people. Here are important events that, like cobblestones that build a road, formed a pathway to freedom during Martin and Mahalia's lifetime. Although great strides have been made, the journey to justice continues.

1911
OCTOBER 26: Mahalia Jackson is born in New Orleans, Louisiana.

1929

JANUARY 15: Martin Luther King Jr. is born in Atlanta, Georgia.

1954
MAY 17: In a unanimous decision in *Brown v. Board of Education of Topeka*, the U.S. Supreme Court rules that segregation in public schools is unconstitutional. Black students and white students are permitted to attend school together.

1955
DECEMBER 1: The Montgomery Bus Boycott begins when Rosa Parks, an active member of the National Association for the Advancement of Colored People (NAACP), refuses to give up her seat to a white passenger on a segregated bus in Montgomery, Alabama.

1956
DECEMBER 21: After a Supreme Court ruling is made, buses in Montgomery are desegregated.

1957
JANUARY AND FEBRUARY: The Southern Christian Leadership Conference (SCLC) is established. Martin Luther King Jr. becomes its first president.

SEPTEMBER 23: Despite being barred by Arkansas Governor Orval Faubus, the "Little Rock Nine," a group of nine black students in Little Rock, Arkansas, enroll in Central High School. To assist in this bold civil rights action, President Dwight D. Eisenhower sends the National Guard to protect the students, who are allowed to enter their school.